MARTIN LUTHER KING, Jr.

A Picture Story

By Margaret Boone-Jones

Illustrations by Roszel Scott

CHILDRENS PRESS, CHICAGO

Library of Congress Catalog Card Number: 68-9483

Martin Luther King, Jr.

There were five in Martin's family. Reverend and Mrs. King were his father and mother. Christine was his big sister, and Alfred was his little brother.

Martin was the one in the middle.

The King family lived in a big house in Atlanta, Georgia.

They were very happy.

Martin's father was a minister. That is why people called him Reverend King.

When the family went to church on Sunday, Martin liked most to listen to his father preach to the people.

He liked the big words that his father used. Martin would say, "I am going to learn to use some big words, too."

Martin was not a tall boy, but he was strong. He liked to play all the games that boys everywhere like to play.

In a football game, he was a very fast runner.

He was one of the best batters on
his block. And he always played to
win.

The King children liked basketball,
too. Their father helped them set up
a basketball court in the backyard.

Martin did not like to fight. He never started a fight. But if he saw a boy teasing a girl or bothering a little child, he would stop him. But he did not stay angry for long. He would make up with the boy and they would be the best of friends.

When Martin, Christine and Alfred were little, they played with all the neighbor children, both black and white. But when they began to go to school, the white children stopped coming to the King's house to play.

Martin noticed that the white boys and girls did not go to the same school that he and Christine and Alfred went to.

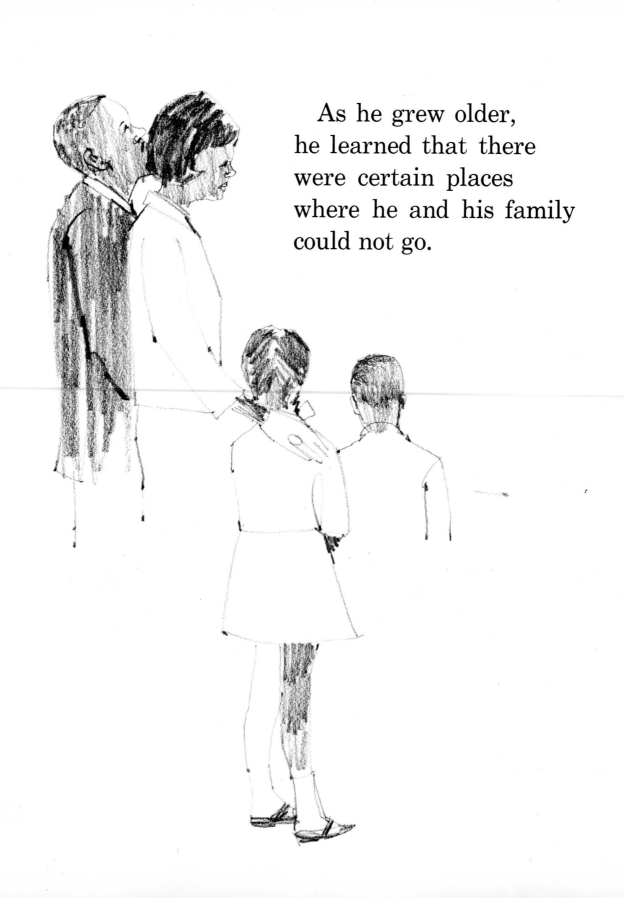

As he grew older,
he learned that there
were certain places
where he and his family
could not go.

These things made Martin very
sad. He wondered what he could do
about them.

He began to think about what he would become when he grew up.

Would he be a doctor and make sick people well?

Would he become a lawyer and help people in court?

Meanwhile, he studied hard in school. He always did more than the teachers asked him to do.

He loved books! He read all the time. Often he spent all his allowance for books, because he liked to own them.

Martin read more and more as he grew older. He liked to read about many different things.

He did so well in school that he finished high school when he was only fifteen. He was still only fifteen when he went away to college.

Do you know what Martin did become when he had finished school?

He was not a doctor.

He was not a lawyer.

He was a minister like his father.

He had found those big words, too.

His words were so beautiful that they made people feel good inside. They made the people want to go right out and do what the words said.

Now Martin was called Reverend King, too.

In the city where Martin Luther King lived, black people could not sit in the front of the bus. They had to sit in the back of the bus. They had to get up and give their seats to white people when the bus was crowded.

Martin said, "That law is not a good law. Perhaps we can have it changed."

"How?" asked the people.

"We will stay off the buses until the law is changed," he said.

"Walk?"

"Yes. Or ride in the cars of friends. Ride in taxis. Do not get into fights, no matter what happens. Be calm. There is a better way of winning than fighting with fists."

Reverend King spoke in beautiful words, telling the black people to love and not to hate. They did as he said. And the buses were almost empty for more than a year. The bus company lost a lot of money.

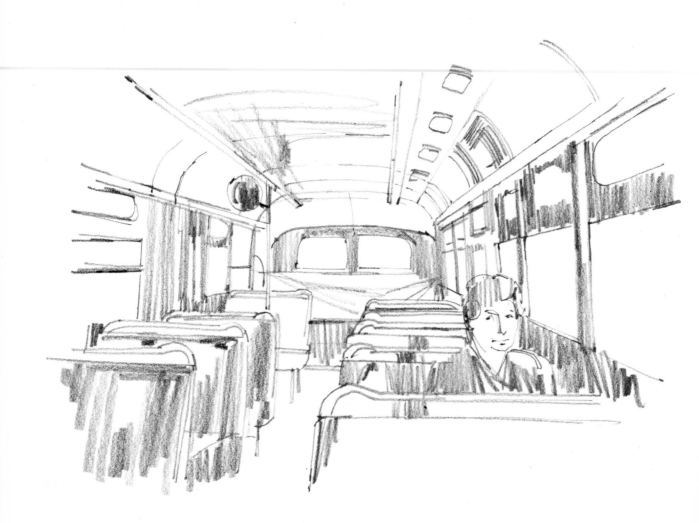

At last the law was changed. All
people could ride and sit wherever
they wished to sit.

Martin Luther King traveled all over the United States and all over the world. He often helped people who were working to have bad laws changed for better ones.

He told people to work for what was right without fighting. And he was always reminding them:

"Be honest. Love each other. Work hard so that you can hold up your heads and be proud of yourselves!"

He became so famous that you could read about him every day in the news. You could hear him on radio and see him on television.

One day in 1964 Martin Luther King was awarded a big prize for doing so many things to bring peace and love among people.

The prize is called the *Nobel Prize*. The winner of a Nobel Prize gets a beautiful medal and a large amount of money.

How do you think Reverend King used the $54,600 that he received?

He did not keep it for himself or his family. He used it to help more and more people.

Then one day in 1968 a terrible thing happened. A man who did not know about love, shot and killed Martin Luther King.

People all over the United States and the world were sad. Many, many hundreds of people went to his funeral. Schools and places of business were closed for the day.

Even though he is gone, Martin Luther King's words and deeds and ideas live on. People can live as he lived, love as he loved, work as he worked. In this way he will never be forgotten.